For the loving arms that hold us high so we can see beyond the fences of our worlds
—K.K.Y.

To Kalia, who has gone beyond the tops of the trees to share her story with the world
—R.W.

Text copyright © 2021 by Kao Kalia Yang
Illustrations copyright © 2021 by Rachel Wada

Carolrhoda Books®
An imprint of Lerner Publishing Group, Inc.
241 First Avenue North
Minneapolis, MN 55401 USA

For reading levels and more information, look up this title at www.lernerbooks.com.

Author's note photo courtesy of Chue Moua. Map by Laura Westlund/Independent Picture Service.

Designed by Emily Harris.
Main body text set in Horley Old Style MT Std.
Typeface provided by Monotype Typography.
The illustrations in this book were created with a combination of traditional mediums, including graphite and watercolor, and digital mediums, including Adobe Photoshop and Procreate.

Library of Congress Cataloging-in-Publication Data

Names: Yang, Kao Kalia, 1980– author. | Wada, Rachel, illustrator.
Title: From the tops of the trees / Kao Kalia Yang ; illustrated by Rachel Wada.
Description: Minneapolis : Carolrhoda Books, [2021] | Audience: Ages 5–9 | Audience: Grades 2–3 | Summary: "A powerful true story of a young girl who has never known life outside a refugee camp and a father determined to help her dream beyond the fences that confine them" —Provided by publisher.
Identifiers: LCCN 2020049356 (print) | LCCN 2020049357 (ebook) | ISBN 9781541581302 | ISBN 9781728430584 (ebook)
Subjects: LCSH: Refugees—Juvenile literature. | Refugee camps—Juvenile literature.
Classification: LCC HV640 .Y368 2021 (print) | LCC HV640 (ebook) | DDC 362.7/7914—dc23

LC record available at https://lccn.loc.gov/2020049356
LC ebook record available at https://lccn.loc.gov/2020049357

Manufactured in the United States of America
1-47329-47956-3/24/2021

FROM THE
TOPS
OF THE
TREES

KAO KALIA YANG

ILLUSTRATED BY **RACHEL WADA**

Carolrhoda Books • Minneapolis

Ban Vinai Refugee Camp, Thailand, 1985

When the sun gets to the highest point in the sky, the leaves of our favorite tree become a great umbrella of cool for my cousins and me to play under.

"Hurry!"

Mai throws a ball of rice onto the ground. Yer races the chickens in the yard to get to it. A bald rooster with black tail feathers beats her. The look on her face is so sad and so hungry the fun disappears.

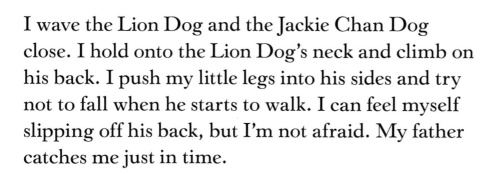

I wave the Lion Dog and the Jackie Chan Dog
close. I hold onto the Lion Dog's neck and climb on
his back. I push my little legs into his sides and try
not to fall when he starts to walk. I can feel myself
slipping off his back, but I'm not afraid. My father
catches me just in time.

In his arms, he lifts me higher and higher.
I squeal.

My father says,
"When someone
falls, you have to
pick them up and lift
them higher than
they were before!"

After a night of heavy rain and wind, we wake to find pebbly fruits scattered on the ground. Beneath our tree, Yer and I crouch low and look for the fruits that are still good enough to eat.

We know that if we eat too many, we'll get stomachaches and our mothers will be mad. If we eat only one or two, we can pretend we're eating hard candy and it is a very special treat.

In the quiet, we can hear the aunties talking about the war as they sew. They talk to each other about the river they had to cross to get to Thailand. They talk to each other about how Thailand wants Hmong refugees to leave their country. They are scared to return to the old country. They are scared to go to a new country. The adults talk of war, and they get scared all over again as if the war was not yet over.

That afternoon I ask my father about the war, and he says, "You're safe."

He takes one of my small hands in his big one and tells me, "Look at your hand." He points down at the tips of my toes and says, "Look at your feet."

He says, "Your hands and your feet will travel far to find peace."

His eyes are as serious as his voice, so I say, "Yes, they will."

It is rations day. Every week, a big truck comes into the empty space in the middle of where we live. Thai soldiers give each family enough food for three days. They tell us they are practicing a "Humane Deterrence Policy" so that no more Hmong people come into the country. I don't know what they are talking about, but I do what the adults around me do and nod my head like I understand.

That evening, before my bath, I look down into the cement well and ask my father why we live behind a gate. I want to know why other people can come in, but we can't leave. He says, "We live in a refugee camp, a place to hold people who are running away from wars."

I ask, "Father, is all of the world a refugee camp?"

"No," he says.

"What is the world outside this camp like?" I ask.

My father has no answers for me.

The next day, as Mai and Yer and I play beneath our tree, my father walks to where my mother and aunties sit sewing. I hear him say, "Chue, can you put Kalia in her nice dress and her hat?"

My mother never allows me to wear them except for pictures.

They lower their voices. Finally, my mother shakes her head, puts down her embroidery, and gets up. She waves her hand for me to follow her.

In our small room where we sleep on a bamboo platform bed on a folded blanket, my mother opens the suitcase where she keeps our nice clothes. She takes out the dress and the hat. She takes out my father's nice shirt and pants. Mother helps me take off my everyday T-shirt and shorts. She wipes me down with the shirt and then tells me to raise my hands over my head.

I feel the cool fabric of the dress fall over my skin. I feel myself growing more and more beautiful with each button she closes at my back. Mother combs my hair before placing the hat on my head. She looks at me carefully and then shakes her head once again and smiles.

Outside, my father is waiting with a camera he's borrowed. When we come out, he puts the camera in my mother's hands.

"I'll change quickly," he says.

In our fine clothes, my father takes me to the tallest tree in the camp. He tells me to close my eyes and hold tight to his neck, to not let go no matter what. Mai and Yer stand at the base of the tree staring at us, hands over their mouths. Even the aunties in the shade take their eyes off the work in their hands to see what we're doing.

I tremble a little as I feel my father climb up the tall tree. I hold as tight to him as I can, tighter than I have even held the Lion Dog or the Jackie Chan Dog. I can feel my heart beating in my eyelids.

At one point, my father slips a little and my mother yells from underneath, but I don't let go and I don't open my eyes.

It is not until my father says, "Look. The world is bigger than this place," that I open my eyes.

I am higher than I have ever been.
A breeze blows and the leaves
shake and I shake with them. My
father says, "Don't be afraid."

I see sky. I see birds flying high. I look down at my mother on the ground. She's run far from the base of the tree, back to the bamboo patio on stilts. There she holds the camera toward us. I see Yer and Mai. The Lion Dog and the Jackie Chan Dog look up at us too, their tails wagging. They are all small and far away.

I look from the houses we live in to the cement well, toward the open field where we get rations, then away from the camp itself, until I see the distant mountains rising at the place where the sky meets the earth. What is on the other side of those mountains?

Another breeze blows, but I don't shake.

"Father, the world is so big," I say.

My father answers, "Yes, it is." He says softly, "One day my little girl will journey far into the world, to the places her father has never been."

My father tells me to smile at the camera, but I can't because I now know that the world is bigger than anything I had imagined. My little legs will have to carry me far.

Author's Note

I was born in the northeastern province of Loei, on the outer edges of Ban Vinai Refugee Camp, in Thailand, on a cool December dawn. I was four years old when my father climbed high into that tree with me. We came to call that photograph my mother took of us *From the Tops of the Trees*. After that first experience, I begged my father to take me to see the world again and again. He asked, "What is your favorite sight from the tops of the trees?" I answered, each time, "Everyone I love and everything I want to remember forever when we leave this place."

When I turned six, my family left the refugee camp behind for a life across an ocean I couldn't possibly see from my father's arms in the treetops. It wasn't only my little legs that I had to rely on, it was buses and planes and the arms of my father and the rest of my family carrying me when I grew tired. Then, to my surprise, those legs grew a little longer and stronger—and just as my father had believed, they did indeed take me far beyond the places he has known.

In my way, I've taken him with me to each place I've been: schools in faraway cities, hotels in strange towns, even up and down mountains whose tops are covered with snow year-round. If you poked a long needle through the globe, from that hot place in the sun where I was born, you'd get to where I am now: a writer who travels all over exploring and learning exactly how big the world can be. I take pictures with my heart for my father.

Now, Mai and Yer and I are all adults. In fact, we have all become mothers. We all have children who we believe will one day see how big and wide the world truly is, and travel to the places we've never been.

Chue is pronounced CHEW. It means *bell* and can be a name for a girl or a boy.

Kalia is pronounced kah-LEE-uh. It refers to the dimples on a face.

Hmong is pronounced MOHNG. The word refers to a people, an ethnic minority, from Southeast Asia. Starting in 1975, many Hmong families came to the United States as refugees of war.

Mai is pronounced MY. It is the most common name for a Hmong girl, and it refers to a young girl or woman.

Yer is pronounced to JHER. It is a name given to the youngest girl and also a polite endearment.

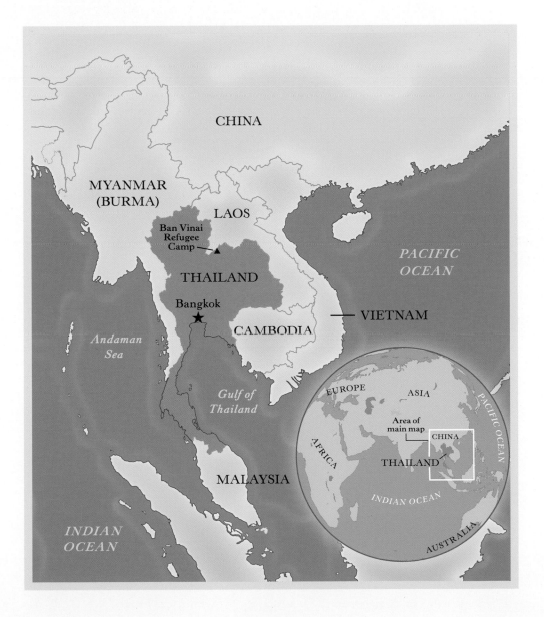